Nurturing
Your Child's
Well-Being

Nurturing
Your Child's
Well-Being

MIDDLE SCHOOL

Trisha DiFazio • Allison Roeser

Publishing Credits

Corinne Burton, M.A.Ed., *President* and *Publisher*
Aubrie Nielsen, M.S.Ed., *EVP of Content Development*
Kyra Ostendorf, M.Ed., *Publisher, professional books*
Véronique Bos, *Vice President of Creative*
Christine Zuchora-Walske, *Senior Editorial Manager*
Alyssa Lochner, *Senior Production Editor*
Ryan Scheife, *Graphic Designer*

Image Credits

All images Adobe Stock, iStock, and/or Shutterstock.

Library of Congress Cataloging-in-Publication Data

LCCN: 2024015414

A division of Teacher Created Materials
5482 Argosy Avenue
Huntington Beach, CA 92649-1039
www.tcmpub.com/shell-education
ISBN 979-8-7659-7725-5
© 2025 Shell Educational Publishing, Inc.

This book is dedicated to parents, guardians, and caregivers who do the hard work and the "heart work" of taking care of children.

Acknowledgments

TD: Thank you to my parents, Peggy and Rocky DiFazio, and to my parents-in-law, Jan and Ken Chapman, for all their love and support. Special thanks to my favorite teacher of all time, my wife, Karen Smith DiFazio. Last but not least, thank you to my coauthor, Allison Roeser, for being one of the best parents and friends that I know.

AR: First and foremost, thank you to Trisha DiFazio for being such an incredible visionary and coauthor and for providing comic relief when it's needed most. Thank you to my parents, John and Deb Roeser, and my siblings, in-laws, and dear friends for their care and kindness. This wouldn't have been possible without Nathan and Luca, who gave me the opportunity to be a parent. A big thanks to Sean for always supporting me.

Huge thanks to all the great people at Teacher Created Materials and Shell Education, especially Christine Zuchora-Walske and Aubrie Nielsen, for making this book possible.

Contents

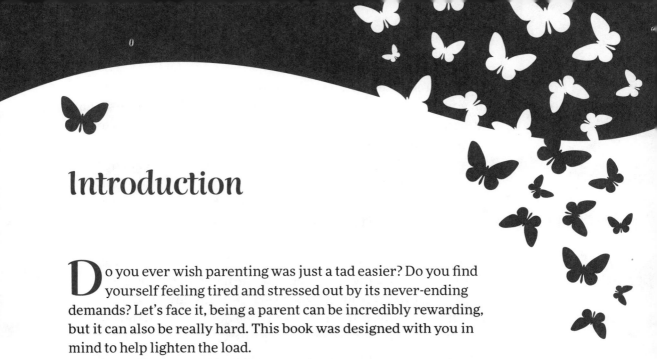

Introduction

Do you ever wish parenting was just a tad easier? Do you find yourself feeling tired and stressed out by its never-ending demands? Let's face it, being a parent can be incredibly rewarding, but it can also be really hard. This book was designed with you in mind to help lighten the load.

We admire and appreciate all that it takes to be a parent these days. Our decades of experience in education and supporting families, along with personal experience in parenting, have shown us time and time again how important social and emotional topics are to daily life. No matter where in the United States we are doing trainings, it all comes back to this: when we can focus on connection and well-being, it helps children and adults grow, feel a sense of belonging, and thrive.

In this book, we offer support and ideas to help make the parenting journey a little easier by providing examples and activities on social and emotional topics that are important to parents and children. We have placed specific emphasis on supporting not only the child but also you, the adult. At the end of the day, one of the best things parents can give a child is a well-regulated adult.

Getting the Most from This Book

Each chapter offers tips, ideas, and activities to support you and your child. We designed the book to be flexible, so you can start on page one and read it through or skip to the chapters that are most relevant for you and your family right now. For example, if you feel like screen time has become a constant battle, check out chapter 6,

Managing Tech Time. Or, if you're looking for new ways to connect with your child, take a look at chapter 4, Creating Connections. That said, as a parent, guardian, or caregiver, you need to be well taken care of too. Therefore, we do suggest you start with the first chapter, Bank on Yourself, which provides ideas for ways to take care of yourself on a daily basis.

You'll get the most out of this book if you fill out the personal inventories, respond to the reflection questions, and use the tips and activities provided. Feel free to use this resource as a workbook, making notes about what works well and adding your own ideas. We've also included digital versions of the inventories and several activities that you can download. (See page 61 for download instructions.) If you're interested in diving a little deeper, callout boxes highlight connections to science and research.

This book is for any parent, guardian, or caregiver parenting children. Parenting is a unique journey for each individual and family, and there is no one-size-fits-all approach. What might work for one child might not work for another. You know your child best! We are not here to tell you how to do anything, but we want to offer ideas that can help along the way. You've got this!

Chapter 1

Bank on Yourself
Parental Self-Care

Parenting is not about perfection; it's about progress. As a parent, you are going to make mistakes. It's okay. Parenting is messy. There isn't one "right" way to parent. Social media might make it look like every second of parenting is fun and easy, but of course that's not true.

Parents want what's best for their children. Turns out, the best thing you can give your child is a calm and present adult. But being calm and present is a lot easier said than done. It requires that you take care of yourself. And when children see their parents taking care of themselves, they feel safe to do so too. **Taking care of yourself is not selfish—it's necessary.**

Deposits and Withdrawals

As a parent, your energy is valuable. One helpful way to conserve energy is by asking yourself this question: *Is this a deposit or a withdrawal?*

What does that mean?

Basically, think of daily activities in terms of deposits and withdrawals. Deposits are things that give you energy, and withdrawals take it away. Everything takes *some* energy, from going to work to cleaning the house. In that way, withdrawals are just a part of life. But people are different, so deposits and withdrawals can vary from parent to parent.

For example, one parent might love cooking dinner because it brings them joy. Engaging in an activity that you enjoy, even a necessary one, is a deposit. However, another parent might dislike cooking dinner. For them, it feels like just one more chore on the to-do list. In that case, it would be a withdrawal.

Making small investments over time can make a big difference. The goal is to understand how these daily activities affect you, so you can focus on making as many deposits as possible. You will have a better chance at making deposits when you carve out time to do so.

Parent Piggy Bank

Identify activities that energize you with the Parent Piggy Bank. This will provide a visual that can serve as a reminder throughout the day. A blank version is available in the digital resources.

Taking a nap
Going for a walk
Listening to my favorite music
Watching my favorite show
Talking with a friend

Always on the Go

The go-go-go of parenting can make it easy to forget an important truth: **Sometimes the most productive thing you can do is rest.** That's right. Read that sentence one more time.

We know it can feel impossible to find time to rest during your busy day. But just because you definitely can't take a thirty-minute nap doesn't necessarily mean you can't take a ten-minute rest, right?

> Stress impacts your nervous system, causing your body to enter a "fight or flight" response. This response releases extra stress hormones called cortisol and adrenaline, which make it more difficult to respond calmly.

Make a Plan

It's easier to make deposits when you plan for them. In the example below, the parent has scheduled time for several deposits. Take a look at your schedule for this week. Where is there time to make

This Week

Monday
9:00 a.m. Meeting
1:30 p.m. Dentist
3:30 p.m. Go for a walk ✓
6:00 p.m. Dance class pickup

Tuesday
8:00 a.m. Bring snack for school
11:00 a.m. PTA meeting
5:30 p.m. After-school pickup

Wednesday
9:00 a.m. Call a friend ✓
5:00 p.m. Grocery shopping

Thursday
7:30 a.m. School carpool
3:00 p.m. Laundry
5:30 p.m. Dinner

Friday
8:30 a.m. Parent-teacher meeting
12:00 p.m. Register for summer camp
5:30 p.m. After-school pickup

Saturday
10:00 a.m. Soccer practice
2:00 p.m. Rest or nap ✓

Sunday
Visiting grandparents
8:00 p.m. Watch a show ✓

deposits? Or are there ways to take away any withdrawals? For example, can you ask for help with cooking or cleaning?

Stress

Stress is a part of life, and it can be a major withdrawal for parents. When you're more stressed, you have less patience for dealing with the day-to-day challenges of parenting. Managing your stress doesn't mean you won't have tough days or lose your cool. However, learning to manage stress will give you the energy you need to show up and be the parent you want to be. Furthermore, the best way to teach your child how to manage stress is to model it for them.

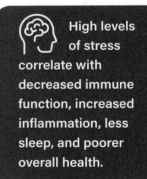 High levels of stress correlate with decreased immune function, increased inflammation, less sleep, and poorer overall health.

You don't need to try to hide your stress from your family. Children actually benefit when they see you cope with stress in a healthy way.

The first step to managing stress is understanding its cause. Think about the questions in the Personal Stress Inventory on the next page to start unpacking your stressors. A downloadable version is available in the digital resources.

☑ Personal Stress Inventory

When do you feel stressed?

What types of things stress you out?

What are you currently doing to manage your stress?

Tips for Managing Stress

There is no one-size-fits-all recommendation when it comes to de-stressing. Everyone is different, so it's important to find what works best for you personally. Each of the activities below can be done solo or with your child.

BREATHE

When life feels like it's moving too fast, deep breathing can help you pump the brakes. Your breath is one of the most effective, powerful ways to relax your body. You can adjust your breath in your car, at home, or at the grocery store.

One example of mindful breathing is called Box Breathing. Give it a try. Picture a square in your mind, and trace around it as you go. Breathe in for four seconds, hold for four seconds, breathe out for four seconds, and rest for four seconds.

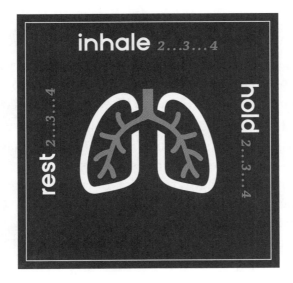

CHECK IN WITH YOUR BODY

Sitting comfortably, take a deep breath in through your nose and let it out through your mouth. As you breathe out, close your eyes. Starting at the top of your head, scan down through your body all the way to your toes. Notice what feels uncomfortable or what areas may need some extra care. Give that stress or tension a color. Now picture a great big magnet pulling the stress out of your body.

MOVE YOUR BODY

Yes, walking, running, and yoga are fantastic ways to move your body. But small movements and stretches can be helpful as well. They can be as simple as rolling your shoulders or unclenching your jaw. Movement is a great way to make a deposit during a busy day.

CALL IN SUPPORT

The saying "it takes a village" is true. Parenting can feel a lot easier when you talk to someone. **Asking for help is not a sign of weakness, it is a sign of strength.**

Here are a few ideas:

- Connect with friends and/or family.
- Reach out to other parents.
- Seek out resources in your school district or community (schools, hospitals, community centers).
- Join online parent support groups.
- Follow social media parenting accounts.

Social media can be a helpful place to get parenting ideas and support. However, it can also be hurtful. If you decide to use social media for parenting advice, here are a few questions to consider:

- Does the content feature an unrealistic lifestyle?
- Does the account share only "perfect" (edited) images?
- Does the message use fear or shame you?
- Does the person have credentials or credible research to back up their message?
- Are you being sold something?
- Do you feel bad about yourself after checking out the content?

Similarly, online support groups can be most useful when they have clear ground rules and are well moderated. Notice how the group is run, what the agreements are, and if the content and environment are supportive.

REFRAME YOUR THOUGHTS

Your thoughts shape your whole day. Making mental deposits starts with being aware of your thinking. Reframing your thoughts is simply looking at them from a different point of view. This is a skill that, with practice, will have a big payoff.

Here are some ideas of simple reframes:

Instead of:	Try:
I'm failing as a parent!	I'm learning as a parent.
I'm a mess!	I'm human.
I can't do this!	I can do hard things.
Why is this happening?	What can I learn from this?
He just wants attention.	He is seeking connection.
She is giving me a hard time.	She is having a hard time.

FOCUS ON WHAT YOU CAN CONTROL

Your time and energy are valuable. Worrying about things you can't control is a withdrawal because it takes a lot of energy. You probably do it all the time without even realizing! It's totally normal. For example, you might worry that others judge your parenting decisions. But you can't control other people's thoughts or opinions. When you focus on what you can control, your energy can be used for deposits.

In my control:

My actions
My goals
Where I focus my attention
How I talk to myself
How I talk to others
What I listen to
and watch

Outside my control:

The past
The future
Other people's beliefs
Other people's opinions
Other people's reactions
Other people's behavior

PRACTICE THE PAUSE

In terms of deposits, practicing the pause is worth its weight in gold. It's like hitting an imaginary pause button that can help your mind and body cool down when you are experiencing big emotions. Taking a moment to pause can make the difference between a hotheaded reaction and a calm response. Next time you feel a big emotion coming on, take three deep breaths and practice the pause.

BE YOUR OWN BESTIE

Imagine that your best friend is late to pick up their child from school. What would you tell them? Now imagine you are late to pick up your child. What would you say to yourself?

Parents often find it easy to be hard on themselves. To make sure you aren't being too harsh, ask yourself these questions:

- Do I forgive myself when I make a mistake?
- Am I flexible when things don't go perfectly?
- Would I let someone talk this way to my best friend?

Showing up as a calm and patient adult is one of the best ways you can support your child. This is certainly easier said than done. Learning how to manage your own stress first will improve your own well-being. Taking this time for yourself ultimately benefits both you and your child. In a world of withdrawals, you deserve to be making deposits too!

 **Chapter 2**

First Things First
Food, Water, Sleep, and Movement

___

When in doubt, get back to basics. Food, water, sleep, and movement are essential for health and overall well-being. It's easy to overlook how much impact these basics have on daily life. Being hungry and tired can be challenging for anyone, including parents. **When your child is having a difficult time, make sure their basics are being met.**

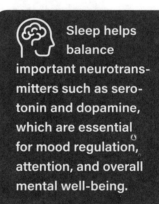 Sleep helps balance important neurotransmitters such as serotonin and dopamine, which are essential for mood regulation, attention, and overall mental well-being.

Children learn habits from the people around them. Modeling healthy habits is one of the best ways to help children develop theirs. Covering the basics starts with adults. Take the inventory below to check in with yourself. (A downloadable version is available in the digital resources.) Then, read on for ways to support your child.

 Back to Basics Parent Inventory
___

Are you eating foods that nourish your body?

Do you exercise or move your body during the day?

Are you getting enough sleep?

Do you drink enough water during the day?

Sleep

Brains and bodies need sleep to function properly. **When children get enough sleep, they can show up as their best selves.** From ages three to five years, kids need ten to thirteen hours of sleep per night. Six- to twelve-year-olds need nine to twelve hours. And young teens thirteen to fourteen years old need eight to ten hours of sleep each night.

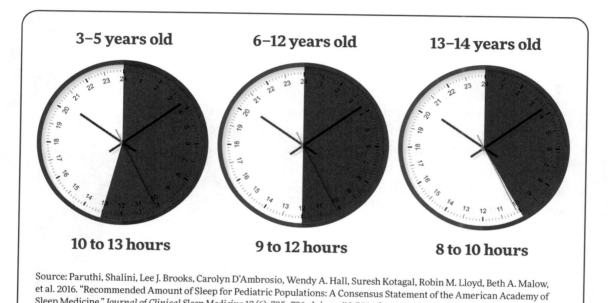

3–5 years old   **6–12 years old**   **13–14 years old**

10 to 13 hours   **9 to 12 hours**   **8 to 10 hours**

Source: Paruthi, Shalini, Lee J. Brooks, Carolyn D'Ambrosio, Wendy A. Hall, Suresh Kotagal, Robin M. Lloyd, Beth A. Malow, et al. 2016. "Recommended Amount of Sleep for Pediatric Populations: A Consensus Statement of the American Academy of Sleep Medicine." *Journal of Clinical Sleep Medicine* 12 (6): 785–786. doi.org/10.5664/jcsm.5866.

Sleep improves many aspects of your child's life, including these:

- Attention
- Behavior
- Learning
- Memory
- Mental health
- Physical health

Falling asleep and staying asleep aren't always easy. Here are some tips to help your child get enough sleep.

5 Tips to Help with Sleep

Set a Regular Bedtime and Wake-Up Time

Try to help your child stick to a sleep schedule as much as you can, within an hour or two, even on the weekends.

Exercise

Regular exercise will help your child sleep better. Do not encourage exercise right before bed, though, because it can create energy and make it harder for your child to fall asleep.

Avoid Caffeine

Caffeine is a stimulant that activates the brain. Make sure your child avoids beverages with caffeine, such as soda, tea, and coffee, after dinner.

Turn Off Electronics

Encourage your child to avoid using screens such as phones, tablets, computers, and TV for at least one hour before going to bed. The light from all these screens can make it harder to fall asleep.

Set the Scene

Try to keep the lights low where the child sleeps as bedtime approaches. Play or suggest your child listen to calming music. Keep their room as cool as possible.

Eat

Food is an essential part of children's health. Choosing healthy and nutritious foods will provide the best fuel for their brains and bodies. Managing emotions and making good decisions is always easier when this basic need is met.

Prioritize these foods for a filling and nutritious diet:

- Vegetables
- Fruits
- Meat and poultry
- Fish and seafood
- Eggs
- Legumes: chickpeas, black beans, lentils, tofu, peanuts
- Dairy: milk, yogurt, cheese, kefir
- Nuts: almonds, cashews, pecans, walnuts, nut butters
- Seeds: hemp, pumpkin, sesame, sunflower, chia, seed butters
- Whole grains: oats, quinoa, barley, rice, whole-grain wheat
- Healthy oils: olive, avocado, sesame

Nutrition plays a crucial role in supporting brain health and function. The food you eat provides the essential nutrients that your brain needs for proper development, maintenance, and optimal performance.

Children can be incredibly picky eaters. It's easy to feel like you've run out of ideas for healthy options. Additionally, it can be challenging to have healthy food available at all times. On the next page you'll find a few suggestions to make healthy eating easier for your family.

5 Tips for Healthier Eating

Plan Ahead

Whether it's Taco Tuesday or Soup Sunday, planning meals in advance can save you time and money. Creating grab-and-go bins in the fridge and pantry makes healthy snacking convenient.

Eat Together

Choosing to eat at a table together can help you and your family stay connected, as well ensure you know what your child is eating.

Give Options

Children feel in control when they are given a choice. Allow children to choose between two healthy foods, like a piece of fruit or cut veggies.

Stock Up on Fruits and Vegetables

It's helpful when the healthy choice is also the easy choice. Keeping a bowl of fruit on the counter for an easy snack can help cut back on less nutritious snacks like chips or candy.

Make Water the Go-To

Encourage water as the go-to beverage. Make sweet drinks like soda, fruit juice, and sports drinks the exception, not the norm.

Drink

Drinking water helps bodies work better by keeping bones, joints, and teeth healthy. Staying hydrated can help improve your child's mood, memory, and attention. Certain factors like levels of activity, heat, and humidity can impact how much water your child needs in order to be hydrated. But for an average day, here are some basic guidelines:

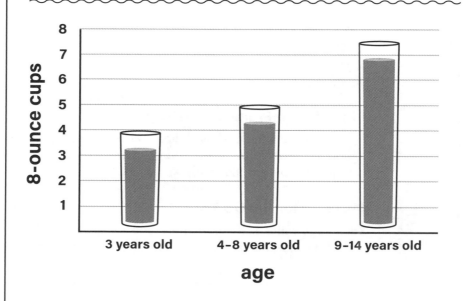

Source: Rethy, Janine. 2020. "Choose Water for Healthy Hydration." American Academy of Pediatrics HealthyChildren.Org. Updated January 27, 2020. healthychildren.org/English/healthy-living/nutrition/Pages/Choose-Water-for-Healthy-Hydration.aspx.

5 Hydration Tips

Pack your child a water bottle.

Have your child log their water in an app.

Give your child a glass of water first thing in the morning.

Add flavor by including slices of cucumber, lemon, lime, or other fruits.

Drink water together.

Move

Whether your child is full of energy or not, movement is good for brain and body development, improves mood, and releases stress.

Movement helps release neurochemicals in the brain that improve motor, social, and cognitive skills.

Children are more likely to move if they're doing things they like. One child might want to learn karate, while another might want to salsa dance. Encourage your child to explore what interests them.

A family movement game is described next. For more movement activities, see chapter 4, Creating Connections.

Four in a Row

Use the movement card provided on the next page (also available in the digital resources) to engage in this active game with your child or children—multiple players can play at once. The aim is to achieve four in a row horizontally, vertically, or diagonally. Players each select four game pieces, such as coins or colored paper, and then decide which actions they'll perform to align their game pieces. Each action is repeated for thirty seconds. To prolong the activity, encourage players to cover the entire card by completing all actions. The goal is to move, challenge yourself and your child, and have fun.

Sleep, water, food, and movement are important parts of a child's health and development. When these needs are met, children can focus better on learning, building strong relationships, and managing their emotions. However, it's common to struggle with keeping these aspects of health engaging and enjoyable. We hope the ideas in this chapter make taking care of these needs more fun and inspiring for both you and your child.

Four in a Row

downward-facing dog	cow	warrior 1	shoulder stand
plank	chair	mountain	bridge
boat	upward-facing dog	horse	tree
cat	child	triangle	bow

Chapter 3

Let's Get Emotional
Understanding Emotions

---

*E*motions are a pattern of body sensations, thoughts, and actions that occur in response to a situation. Emotions are a reaction, and they in turn can cause physiological (body) and psychological (mind) reactions. This circular nature of emotions is why people sometimes get swept up by them, and it's especially easy for this to happen with young people. That's why it's important for both children and their parents to understand emotions and how they affect others.

As a parent, when was the last time you felt a strong emotion? How did you express it?

Not everyone is comfortable talking about emotions. But children and adults are more successful at managing emotions when they are able to label and express how they feel. You can help your child by having a home environment where emotions are discussed, labeled, and understood. **When you know better, you can do better.**

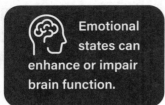

Emotional states can enhance or impair brain function.

Six Facts about Emotions

1. Emotions come and go.
2. Emotions provide important information.
3. It's normal to have many different emotions.
4. Bottling up emotions can have a negative impact.
5. Children learn to express and manage their emotions from the adults around them.
6. Emotions affect bodies.

Teens and Emotions

Remember being a teenager? Was any of it easy? Probably not. Teens go through big physical changes that affect their moods, interests, and needs. These changes can impact their social and emotional health. Mood swings and intense emotions are to be expected during the teen years. As a parent, help them manage these big emotions in a positive way. Teens can feel consumed by their emotions. Help them remember that a bad day doesn't mean a bad life.

Body Clues

Emotions can affect people's bodies in different ways. For example, some people experience anxiety in the stomach. So, if a child is anxious, and they don't have the ability to express that, they might say that they have a stomachache. You might notice that when you're mentally feeling well, your body feels relaxed, refreshed, and able to focus. When you start to get upset, you may notice that you clench

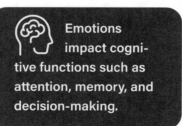

Emotions impact cognitive functions such as attention, memory, and decision-making.

your jaw, your heart starts pounding, or you start to sweat. As a parent, it's helpful to keep an eye out for the clues and to pay attention to how your own emotions can impact you physically. If you understand how emotions show up in your body, it will be easier to understand how they show up in your child's.

The Importance of Identifying Emotions

Parents who can speak with their children about emotions help their children develop emotional intelligence and understand their own emotions better. Children often don't know how to express their feelings. Instead, they communicate their feelings through their behavior. **Behind every behavior is a need.**

For example, if a child is feeling ignored, they might need connection. But if they don't have the language to express that need, they might act out in a way that cannot be ignored. Maybe they throw a chair, cut their bangs, or have a meltdown. The child might feel that negative attention is better than none at all. You can help your child find the words to express their emotions instead of acting out in moments of needing connection. Learning and improving upon these communication skills will help your child throughout their entire life.

Labeling our emotions helps us:

Emotions Word Wheel

To help get children talking about emotions, use the Emotions Word Wheel on the next page (also available in the digital resources). With your child, go through each of the words on the wheel, starting with the inner ring first and working your way out. For each word, you can take turns, asking your child to explain what they think the word means and then giving your own definition. You can also ask them how the different emotions feel in their body. Once your child has more familiarity with each of the words, you can make it a game:

- Take turns acting out or playing charades with a specific emotion.
- Match an emotion from the wheel to the emotion of a character when watching a movie or TV show or reading a book.
- Draw, color, or dance an emotion.

As your child becomes more comfortable with naming emotions, you can ask them to use any of the words to describe their own emotions in a situation.

Emotions Word Wheel

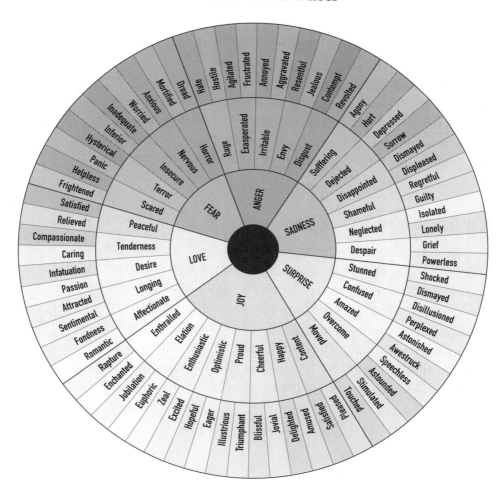

Emoji Check-In

This check-in chart (also available in the digital resources) offers a quick and easy way to check in with children. Ask your child to share or point to the emoji they are feeling.

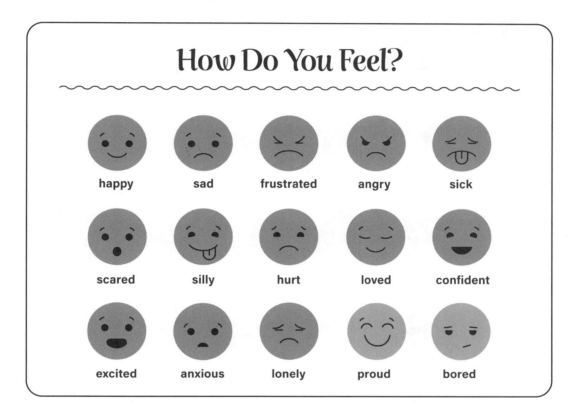

How Do You Feel?

happy · sad · frustrated · angry · sick

scared · silly · hurt · loved · confident

excited · anxious · lonely · proud · bored

Managing Emotions

The first step to managing emotions is identifying them. When you know what you're feeling, it's easier to deal with it. Same goes for your child. No one is born knowing how to handle their emotions; it's something people learn. Even for grown-ups, it can be tough! But remember, like any skill, it gets easier with time and practice.

All feelings are okay, but all behavior isn't. While it's normal to have emotions such as anger, frustration, or worry, sometimes

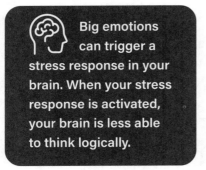

Big emotions can trigger a stress response in your brain. When your stress response is activated, your brain is less able to think logically.

they can lead to harmful behavior. Your goal should be to communicate your understanding of emotions, but also to be clear about what safe behavior is. For example: "It's okay that you're angry, but it's not okay to hit your sister."

It's common for children to have big emotions and cry. In those moments, the crying can impact the adult too. You might have noticed that telling someone to calm down rarely calms them down. Similarly, telling your child to stop crying may not help them actually stop crying. Here are some other things you can say in the moment.

That was scary (or surprising or sad).

It's okay to feel sad or upset.

I'm here to listen when you're ready to talk.

It's okay to cry.

I love you.

I hear you.

I'm here to help.

Would you like a hug?

The point of these phrases isn't to teach children not to have difficult emotions, but *how* to have them. For example, your aim should not be to teach children never to be angry, but to teach them how to express and manage that anger in a healthy way. Everyone experiences a range of emotions. No child wants to have a meltdown. It's not fun. Big behaviors are the result of big feelings. When children are feeling intense emotions, they need help, not punishment. One way to help children calm down is to help them focus on their breathing and senses.

Calming Countdown

This is a great way to help children calm down or de-stress by focusing on their five senses. Have your child walk through each of the prompts on the images below during moments of intense emotion.

Name five things you see.

Name four things you hear.

Name three things you smell.

Name two things you are touching.

Name one thing you taste.

Breathing Strategies

Here are some breathing strategies to manage strong emotions. It's helpful to model them for your child first. You can then do them together with your child—or on your own. Practice them together when you're feeling calm, so you'll both be ready and able to use them when you're having big emotions.

Breathe and Count

Tell your child to breathe in while counting to four and then exhale while counting to four. Then have them pick any number and experiment with how many seconds they can inhale and exhale for.

Shoulder Roll Breath

Have your child roll their shoulders up toward their ears while inhaling deeply. Then they should breathe out through their mouth and roll their shoulders down and back.

4-3-5 Breathing

Breathe in for four counts, hold for three, and breathe out for five.

Peaceful Place

Tell your child to close their eyes and take a relaxing breath. Say, "You are going to build an imaginary hideaway in your mind. Imagine you are in a peaceful place. Now add some details that make you happy. Imagine doing something fun like flying through the air or riding a whale." When you are finished, have your child say goodbye to their peaceful place and remind them they can always come back.

What Helps Me Wheel

Here's an activity you can do with your child when you have a little more time. During a calm moment, have your child identify things that are helpful to them in times of stress. Children will likely need some help coming up with options. Feel free to create your own personal What Helps Me Wheel also. A visual reminder is helpful for children and adults.

Above is an example of a completed wheel. Your child's may include some of these things, but it should be specific to them. (A blank version follows. It is also available in the digital resources, in multiple versions allowing space for a few or many answers.)

What Helps Me Wheel

Directions: Draw or write about what helps you.

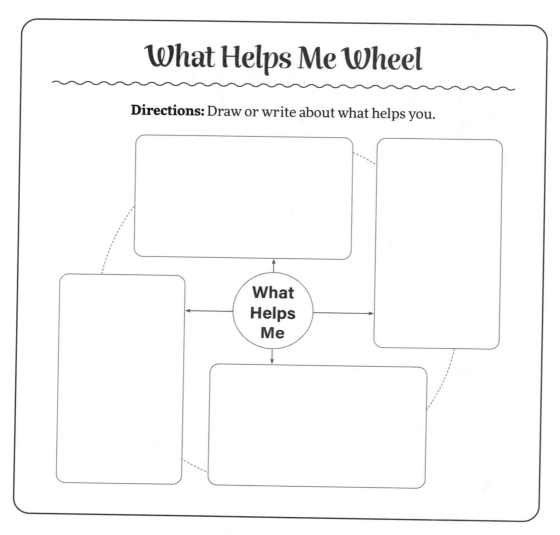

What
Helps
Me

It Starts with Us

Children learn to manage their emotions from the adults around them. It can be hard not to get swept up in your child's emotions. Children learn more from what parents do than from what they say. The best way to help your child manage their emotions is to first manage your own. Using the Parent Emotional Management Inventory on the next page, choose the column that best describes where you're at with managing your own emotions. (The chart is also available in the digital resources.)

✓ Parent Emotional Management Inventory

	I don't know what this means.	I'm on my way, but I could use a little help.	I'm pretty good at this.
I can identify my emotions.			
I can effectively manage my emotions.			
I have tools and strategies to help myself during a difficult time.			

STOP

Strong emotions can lead to strong reactions. Pausing in a situation helps you choose how to respond rather than reacting automatically. Try the STOP strategy below. Although we've included this strategy for you as the parent, you can also teach it to your child.

S—Stop. Remember to pause.
T—Take a few breaths.
O—Observe what you are feeling or thinking at the moment.
P—Proceed by *choosing* how you want to respond, rather than reacting without thought.

When children feel angry or worried, their brains struggle to focus on learning, reasoning, or thinking logically. Secure relationships with parents or caregivers help children develop better skills to regulate their emotions. It's important to remember that learning to manage emotions takes time, and brains need assistance to calm down when facing frustration or intense feelings. But with the right tools and practice, both children and adults can learn to identify and manage emotions effectively.

Chapter 4

Creating Connections

Relationship Building with Your Child

C hildren do better when they feel connected to adults. At the same time, parenting is a full-time job. Your to-do list can feel a mile long. It's easy to get distracted and miss out on opportunities to connect with your children. The good news is that quality time does not need to be expensive or time-consuming. What children really want is their parents' attention. Ask yourself the following questions (also available in the digital resources) before digging into our suggestions.

 Parent-Child Connection Inventory

What are some ways you like to connect with your child?

How does your child like to spend time with you?

What times of day or daily activities feel like opportunities to connect with your child (mornings, after school, evenings, mealtimes, car rides)?

Talk

Talking is one of the fastest and easiest ways to connect with your child. Whether you need help starting a conversation or guiding it, here are a few fun ideas.

Checking In

Children don't always know how to tell adults how they are doing. Sometimes they might not even know how they feel about something until you ask them.

BATTERY LIFE

The concept of battery life helps children understand their own energy level. You can explain that "battery life" means how much energy (physically or emotionally) they have, on a scale from 0 percent to 100 percent. Simply asking, "What's your battery life?" can give you a better understanding of how they are feeling.

ROSE, BUD, THORN

Teach your child this strategy. Then you can ask all three questions for a longer check-in, or just one for a quick conversation.

- Rose: What's something good that happened today?
- Bud: What's something you are looking forward to?
- Thorn: What's a challenge you are dealing with?

Quick Connections

These conversation starters can create connections in the car, in line at the grocery store, or at mealtimes.

QUESTIONS TO REPLACE "HOW WAS YOUR DAY?"

- What made you smile or laugh today?
- Was there anything that was hard today?
- What is something you want me to know?
- What was your favorite thing you did at school today?
- If you could choose who you sit next to at school, who would you pick?
- If you could be a teacher for a day, what subject or topic would you choose to teach?
- If your mood were a type of weather, what would it be? Would it be sunny, cloudy, stormy, or something else?

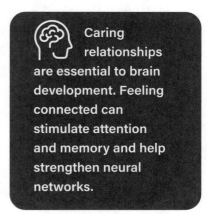

Caring relationships are essential to brain development. Feeling connected can stimulate attention and memory and help strengthen neural networks.

WOULD YOU RATHER

Would you rather . . .

- Have three one-month breaks from school, or one three-month break? Why?
- Live alone in a huge house or live in a normal-size house with fifty roommates? Why?
- Replace your toothpaste with salsa or replace your shampoo with hot sauce? Why?
- Be the president of the nation or a professional athlete? Why?
- Eat a bug or a worm? Why?

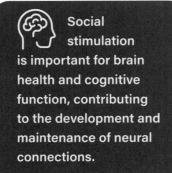

Social stimulation is important for brain health and cognitive function, contributing to the development and maintenance of neural connections.

Play

Children learn through playing. It's one of the best things they can do to grow and develop. Playing with your child for even five minutes a day will make the relationship stronger. And, bonus—children are more willing to listen to their parents if they've spent some time together beforehand. Here are some ways to play with your child.

- Play their favorite video or board game
- Learn a card game
- Do a scavenger hunt
- Play charades
- Play tag
- Go to a park
- Do a nature walk
- Play Name That Tune
- Play Memory
- Play Two Truths, One Lie

Create

Children love being creative. Offering them different options to create will help focus their energy and give you both something to do together. Here are some suggestions for getting creative with your child.

- Paint
- Sing
- Cook or bake
- Make a family time capsule
- Put on a fashion show
- Create marshmallow-and-toothpick structures
- Do at-home science experiments
- Make a personalized word search
- Make vision boards
- Build something

Move

Children love to move. They need to be able to get their energy out. Here are some ways to help your child move without ruining the furniture.

- Learn/make a TikTok dance
- Volunteer
- Do a house project
- Go for a walk
- Hand-wash a car
- Work in the yard
- Take a bike ride
- Play Freeze Dance
- Play balloon volleyball (or regular volleyball!)
- Make and complete an obstacle course

Chill Out

Rest is essential for children's health. Both parents and children benefit from having downtime during the day. Here are some ways you can connect while winding down together.

- Read
- Do mindfulness and breathing exercises
- Draw
- Color
- Listen to relaxing music
- Listen to a story or podcast
- Do a puzzle
- Watch a show
- Journal
- Stretch

Starting the Day

Morning routines that involve connecting with each other help set the tone for the day. Here are a few ideas to kick-start the morning with connection:

- Show affection
- Say good morning and make eye contact
- Take a few deep breaths together
- Eat breakfast together
- Bring them a glass of water
- Play calming music
- Pack school lunch or snacks together

Ending the Day

After a long day, evening routines that include connection help end the day on a strong and positive note. Bedtime provides a wonderful opportunity to share quality time with your child. Bedtime routines can have their challenges, but it helps when your child looks forward to bedtime as a chance to connect with you. Here are a few ideas:

- Ask questions about a topic they like
- Have them show you something they are interested in
- Let them ask you questions
- Talk about something that happened in your day
- Give a kiss, hug them, or rub their back
- Read together
- Listen to a podcast or music together

My Favorite Things Game

Make a list of your favorite things. Have your child make a list of theirs. You can use the form below (also available in the digital resources) if you'd like. Take turns guessing each other's answers. This can lead to a discussion about similarities and differences. The goal is to learn more about each other and use that information to connect at a deeper level.

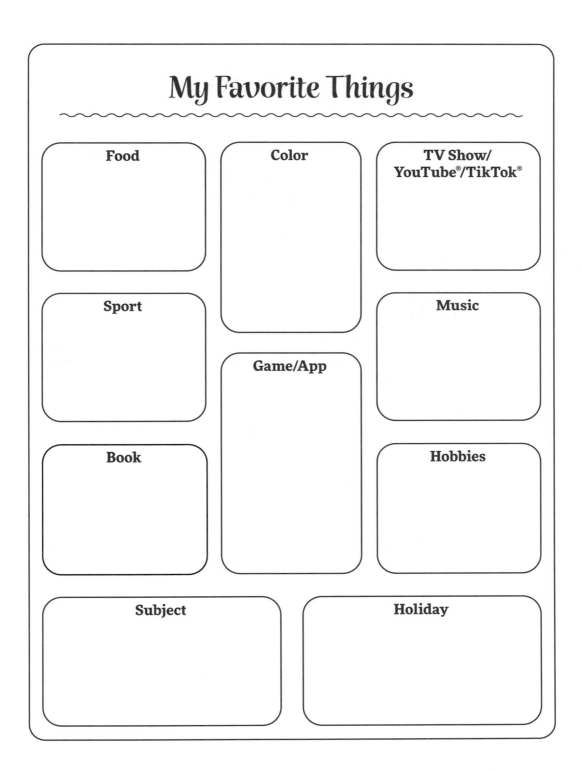

My Favorite Things

Food

Color

TV Show/YouTube®/TikTok®

Sport

Music

Game/App

Book

Hobbies

Subject

Holiday

Let Your Silly Flag Fly

Finally, don't be afraid to get goofy. Whether it's a secret handshake or a thirty-second dance party, children always appreciate it when adults let their silly flags fly.

Humans are wired for connection. Caring relationships are essential to your child's development. Consistently connecting with your child helps them feel safer, more confident, and more secure. Remember, no parent gets it right all the time, so ask for help when you need it or simply give yourself a break.

Chapter 5

Making the Most of Mistakes
Helping Create a Growth Mindset

Mistakes are a normal part of life. Everyone makes mistakes. Making a mistake doesn't make you a bad person—it makes you a human. **Fun fact: mistakes play an important part in helping brains grow.**

Mistakes come in all shapes and sizes. They can be stressful, frustrating, and even downright painful. But the important thing is that mistakes can turn into valuable lessons when you are willing to learn from them. Sometimes, children worry so much about making mistakes that they stop trying altogether. When they give up, they miss out on opportunities to learn and grow their brains.

Take a moment to reflect on your past mistakes using the following inventory (also available in the digital resources).

 Parent Mistakes Inventory

What were some mistakes that you made when you were young?

How were mistakes treated when you were young?

What's a recent mistake you've learned from?

Growth Mindset

Having a growth mindset means seeing challenges and mistakes as opportunities to learn and improve. Encouraging a growth mindset in your child helps them face challenges and learn from their mistakes. When you show your child that their abilities can be developed by hard work and dedication, it makes them more resilient. It also helps them take chances and go outside their comfort zone, even if it feels a little scary. Believing in the potential for improvement can boost motivation.

The examples below are some simple ways to help your child reframe their thinking from a fixed mindset to a growth mindset.

Fixed Mindset

Growth Mindset

I'll never understand this.

This is too hard.

I give up.

I can't do it right.

Mistakes help me learn.

I can't do this yet.

I can ask for help.

I can try another way.

The Power of "Yet"

The small change from "I can't do this" to "I can't do this YET" reminds children that the door to learning the skill is still open. It helps them keep in mind that they can learn and grow with practice and effort.

Five Ways to Manage Mistakes

Here are a few ways to respond when mistakes happen. It's helpful when you can model these strategies for your child.

1. Redo It

A redo is a great way to say, "Let's try that again." Whenever possible, give your child a redo after a mistake.

2. Own It

Help your child take responsibility for the mistakes they've made and what they've learned from their mistakes.

3. Praise It

Encourage and praise children when they admit their mistakes. Applaud their hard work and bravery in facing challenges.

4. Repair It

Show your child how to apologize when their mistakes have hurt others.

5. Reframe It

Help children look at the good side of getting things wrong. Help them see the value in making mistakes and then learning from them.

Pros and Cons

Helping children make responsible decisions is a big part of the growing and learning process. The following activity helps you talk through the pros and cons of a decision with your child.

At the top of a chart, write the question or scenario. Next, list the positives or advantages of the decision in the Pros column. Do the same with the negatives or disadvantages of the decision in the Cons column. Use this visual to talk through different options and come to a decision. For an example, see "Trying Out for the Basketball Team" below.

Trying Out for the Basketball Team

Pros	Cons
Learn new skills	Feel sad if I don't make the team
Get regular exercise	Less free time after school
Play on a team	Could get hurt
Make new friends	

SODAS

Making responsible decisions is a skill. Like all skills, it takes time and practice to learn. SODAS is a strategy that helps your child really think about their decisions and the consequences of their actions. SODAS stands for Situation, Options, Disadvantages, Advantages, and Solution. Ask your child to identify a situation in which they have to make a decision. Using the chart on the next page, come up with a few options and talk through the advantages and disadvantages of each until you reach a solution. A blank chart is available in the digital resources.

Making mistakes and learning to make good decisions are natural parts of everyday life. Often, human brains are inclined to dwell on mistakes or make them feel bigger than they are. A growth mindset helps reduce these inclinations. Additionally, a growth mindset is important for children's success, as it fosters resilience and perseverance. With support and guidance, you can help your child develop a growth mindset, which can enhance their academic performance and emotional well-being.

SODAS Chart

~~~~~~

Directions: Complete the chart to make your decision.

Situation   **O**ptions   **D**isadvantages   **A**dvantages   **S**olution

Situation:

Option 1	Option 2	Option 3
Disadvantages	**Disadvantages**	**Disadvantages**
1.	1.	1.
2.	2.	2.
3.	3.	3.

Option 1	Option 2	Option 3
Advantages	**Advantages**	**Advantages**
1.	1.	1.
2.	2.	2.
3.	3.	3.

Solution:

Chapter 6

Managing Tech Time

Helping Children with Their Screens and Devices

No one has a perfect relationship with screen time. There is no judgment here. Whether it's cell phones, smartwatches, tablets, or TVs—technology is all around us. This can make managing screen time for children feel like a constant battle. And it's not only about how long they are watching but *what* they are watching that you want to pay attention to.

The first step in managing tech for your child is managing tech for yourself. When parents model responsible tech use, children are more likely to do the same. Take the Parent Screen Time Inventory on the next page (also available in the digital resources) to see how you are doing with tech.

> The prefrontal cortex, responsible for decision-making and impulse control, is one of the last parts of the brain to mature. It isn't fully developed until the mid-to-late twenties. This can make it challenging for children and adolescents to regulate the urge to continuously watch, play, or interact with digital content.

Parent Screen Time Inventory

How much time do you spend on screens in a day?

Do you feel like you have a healthy balance of screen time?

What would you like to change about your screen time?

Ten Tips for Managing Screen Time

1. Give Them the "Why"

Technology is not the enemy. You should simply aim to help your child find the right balance between screen time and other activities. **Children respond to rules and restrictions better when they understand the reasons behind them.** Talk to your child about why managing screen time is important and also how it benefits them. When creating rules about screen time, involve everyone in the family so they feel included. It's also a good idea to revisit any rules or goals every so often to make sure everyone is on the same page.

2. Set the Example

As a parent, you are your child's first and best teacher. As with everything else, your child is looking to you to see how you interact with technology. When your child sees you following your own rules, they are more likely to follow suit. Healthy limits start with providing a good example.

3. Make It a Team Effort

When children first start using devices, they will need your help and supervision. They shouldn't be on the internet by themselves because they can easily find things that are inappropriate or dangerous. Be curious about which sites and apps they engage with. Try watching things together. Being involved when your child is young will help lay the foundation for the guidance they need on social media when they get older.

4. Set Expectations

Create clear agreements with your child on how much screen time is allowed. Being clear and consistent will make everyone's life easier. You will probably get some pushback in the beginning, but it will get smoother over time. If your child is used to spending a lot of time on screens, you can start with small changes—baby steps.

5. Have a Routine

Routines give children a sense of control and help them know what to do and when to do it. Children feel more confident and secure when they know what's coming. For example, you might allow your child a set amount of screen time after school, but dinnertime is a screen-free zone.

6. Create Screen-Free Zones

These zones can be times or places. The dinner table can be designated the screen-free zone, or the hour before bedtime. Also, it helps if devices are out of sight in order to help them stay out of mind during screen-free times. Additionally, you might try storing all child tech devices in the same place after a bedtime handover.

7. Prepare for the Shutdown

Imagine being in the middle of an important text message and someone takes your phone out of your hand. That is how it can feel for children when parents shut off their devices with no transition time. Giving them time to shut down and exit their apps or games will allow them to finish what they're doing and save their progress.

8. Use Parental Controls

Each app or device has parental control settings, which are designed to monitor or limit a child's access. However, parental controls aren't foolproof and will still require your active involvement. Children can often navigate around these settings. Combine parental control and open communication for the best online safety results.

9. Offer Alternatives

Children benefit from having a variety of online and offline experiences. Healthy screen time management includes prioritizing real-life experiences and connections over online ones. When asking your child to stop using their device, it's helpful to have an alternative activity. After screen time is up, you can share other options such as playing outside, doing a puzzle, or cooking. You can also let them be bored—it's good for their brain.

10. Prioritize Quality

Tech content can vary in quality. Some content can be helpful with learning and development, and some can be harmful. Check the age and content ratings to make sure the content is age appropriate. Discussing each app and having clear communication about what sites are allowed will support your child in making better decisions.

Staying Safe

Here are a few things to teach your child so they stay as safe as possible online.

Open-Door Policy. You can't monitor your child 24/7, so one of the best tools to keep them safe is the knowledge that they can come to you with any questions or concerns about what they find online.

Think Before You Post. Explain that once something is posted online, it often can't be erased or deleted completely. Your child should not post anything they wouldn't want their parents, teachers, or future employers to see.

Don't Get Personal. Remind your child to avoid sharing personal information. Things like phone numbers, addresses, current locations, or pictures of the exterior of where they live should never be posted online.

No Strangers. Tell your child to ignore texts, messages, or requests from strangers. They should chat only with people they know.

Keep Track of Passwords. Your child should share passwords only with family members.

Don't Take the Bait. Children should not click links, open attachments, or accept gifts from any unknown source.

Mental Health Concerns

The pull of technology is undeniable, and in a lot of cases, it can be downright addictive. Adults can struggle with their technology habits. For young people, the challenges can be even greater because of where they are developmentally. For that reason, phones and social media come with a variety of mental health impacts to consider before allowing your children to engage.

Social Media and Self-Esteem

Smartphone use, along with social media, can contribute to feelings of loneliness and low self-esteem among young people. As the rate of social media use has increased, there has also been an increase in anxiety, depression, and mental distress among children and adolescents.

This can be particularly worrying because the tween and adolescent years are a time of great uncertainty and vulnerability for young people. They feel a desire to fit in, be accepted by peers, and understand their place in the world. The craving for positive feedback can create in young people a vicious cycle of posting on social media hoping for more likes and validation.

Social media often negatively affects the way young people see themselves due to their natural tendency to compare themselves to others. Social media, in addition to various apps, filters, and advertising, can create or display unrealistic images of beauty. Exposure to social media for children and adolescents often creates a desire to change their appearance (such as face, hair, or skin) and increases body image concerns and disordered eating.

Social Media, Gaming, and Social Development

Social media can also ramp up a sense of envy and fear of missing out (FOMO) when young people see peers or influencers portray a certain lifestyle or only highlight all the great things going on in their lives. This leads to increased stress, and young people may mistakenly think that others in their social network are better off— even if that isn't the case.

When children spend more time in front of screens, it means they are spending less time in person with peers and family members. Non-screen-based activities such as sports, socializing, homework, reading books, and even doing chores are critical for brain development and boosting creativity and physical activity. These non-screen activities protect against the potentially negative effects of too much screen time.

While various apps and social media platforms may attempt to monitor inappropriate content, there is no realistic way all content can be accounted for. That's why it's important to understand that anytime children are on social media, gaming, or on other internet-based content platforms, they may be exposed to information that is not appropriate for their age.

Cyberbullying

Cyberbullying is when someone uses technology to harass, threaten, or embarrass another person. It can take place through any social media platform, any messaging platform, any app or website with a social component, and any video game played communally. Cyberbullying might be a comment, text, or post that is directly mean or hurtful. It can also be less obvious, like posting personal information, videos, or pictures to hurt and embarrass another person. Perpetrators can make fake accounts or screen names to harass others. Experiencing cyberbullying can leave children and teenagers with lower self-esteem, less interest in school, lower grades, and mental health struggles such as anxiety and depression.

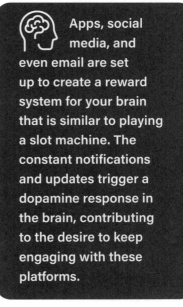 Apps, social media, and even email are set up to create a reward system for your brain that is similar to playing a slot machine. The constant notifications and updates trigger a dopamine response in the brain, contributing to the desire to keep engaging with these platforms.

SIGNS YOUR CHILD MAY BE EXPERIENCING CYBERBULLYING

- They act overly emotional after using a device.
- They delete their social media accounts.
- They experience drastic changes to mood.
- They become nervous when receiving texts or notifications.
- They withdraw from family or friend groups.

WHAT TO DO IF YOUR CHILD HAS EXPERIENCED CYBERBULLYING

- Reassure your child that it's not their fault.
- Report it to law enforcement, school, or the platform where the bullying is occurring.
- Block the bully.
- Seek support from outside sources such as mental health professionals or school counselors.
- Help manage stress by doing fun activities.

WHAT TO DO IF YOUR CHILD IS PARTICIPATING IN CYBERBULLYING

- Acknowledge the issue and take steps to ensure the cyberbullying does not continue
- Remain calm.
- Keep an open line of communication with your child.
- To understand the root of the problem, ask your child questions.
- Help your child understand how the person being bullied may feel.

Technology Agreements

One thing that can help conversations around technology guidelines is to come up with an agreement. As with any agreement, the main idea is to work together and be open to input when introducing the idea. Check out the sample agreement on the next page to get started. A blank version is available in the digital resources. And remember, even if your child already has a device, it's never too late to set boundaries and reestablish rules that best support their safety and mental health.

Sample Completed Technology Agreement

Time Limits

☑ I ___Elizabeth___ agree to the following guidelines for safe use of technology.

☑ I will turn off devices _1_ hr before bed.

☑ I am allowed _1_ hour(s) of screen time per day.

Content and Sharing

Apps and websites that I am allowed to use: _Khan Academy, Duolingo, GarageBand_

Apps and websites that I am not allowed to use: _Instagram and Snapchat_

I can play games that are rated:

☑ E (everyone)

☑ E10+ (everyone 10 and older)

❑ T (teen)

❑ M (mature)

❑ AO (adults only)

❑ RP (rating pending)

Video games that I am allowed to play at my home, or anyone else's home:

Minecraft, Mario Kart, The Legend of Zelda, Forza

Safety

I am:

☑ Responsible for what I do and say online.

I understand:

☑ That anything I say, share, or send can be made public, even if I am sending to close friends.

I will:

☑ Follow the rules my parents set for online activities.

☑ Share my passwords only with my parents or caregivers for all social media accounts.

☑ Tell my parents if I feel I am being mistreated, teased, or bullied online.

I will not:

☑ Share personal information about myself, family, or friends online.

☑ Mistreat, tease, or bully any other person online.

☑ Text, interact, or meet up with people online that I do not know.

Consequences

I understand that breaking our agreement will lead to the following

consequences: __Losing all screen time for two weeks.__

Child's signature _____ Elizabeth Doe _____

Parent signature _____ John Doe _____

Technology is a part of life for both you and your child. Learning to navigate all the technology your child is interested in takes time, practice, and patience. Rest assured that you have what it takes to help your child develop a healthy relationship with technology.

We're rooting for you as you nurture your child's social and emotional well-being. There is no one-size-fits-all approach when it comes to parenting. Take it one step at a time and pick the activities that appeal to you. Last, but certainly not least, be kind to yourself in the process!

Accessing the Digital Resources

To download the reproducible forms for this book, visit **go.freespirit.com/nurture-ms**.

About the Authors

 **Trisha DiFazio,** M.A.T., is an author, education consultant, and professional screenwriter. With over two decades of dedicated work in the field of education, she brings a wealth of experience, having served as classroom teacher and adjunct professor at the University of Southern California. She holds a master of arts in teaching from National Louis University, an ESL Endorsement from Dominican University, and International TEFL Certification. Trisha is passionate about empowering individuals and organizations through social-emotional learning and mindfulness.

 **Allison Roeser,** M.H.S, P.C.C., is an author, leadership coach, and education consultant specializing in social-emotional learning. She has almost two decades of experience working with leaders in education, child welfare, and social change. Allison holds a master of health science degree from Johns Hopkins University and a Professional Coach Certification through the International Coach Federation. Previously, Allison served as deputy director at Westat, a research organization where she directed studies focused on health and education.

Trisha and Allison are coauthors of *Social-Emotional Learning Starts with Us: Empowering Teachers to Support Students.* They are also cofounders of SEL&Beyond, an organization dedicated to providing professional development that is engaging, inspiring, and fun.